LIFE **ON EARTH!**
Biodiversity Explained

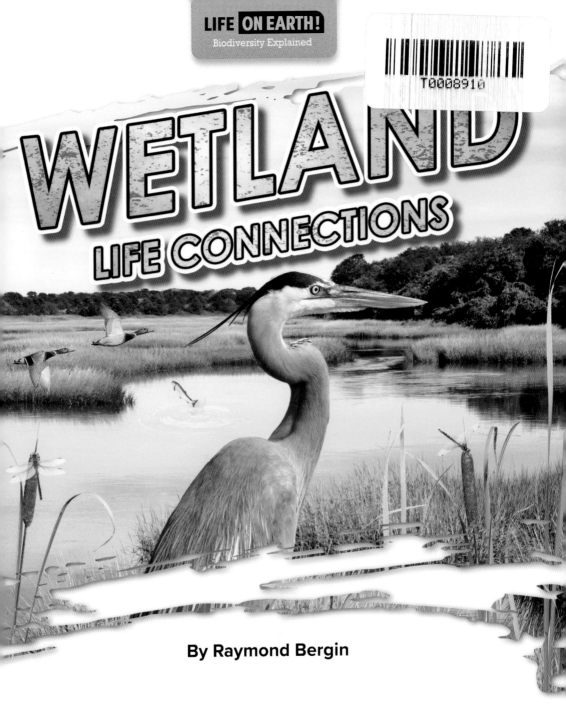

WETLAND
LIFE CONNECTIONS

By Raymond Bergin

BEARPORT
PUBLISHING

Minneapolis, Minnesota

Credits

Cover and title page, © Mark Kostich/iStock, © KenWiedemann/iStock, © Anagramm/iStock, © Somchai Sookkasem/iStock, © Krasowit/Shutterstock, © alslutsky/Shutterstock, and © Artiste2d3d/Shutterstock; 4–5, © Irina Wilhauk/Shutterstock; 6–7, © Rosanne Tackaberry/Alamy; 8–9, © Khaichuin Sim/Getty Images; 10, © Adisak Mitrprayoon/iStock; 11T, © HelloRF Zcool/Shutterstock; 11B, © Dorota Przesmycka/Shutterstock; 12–13, © Cavan Images/Getty Images; 13, © jferrer/iStock; 14, © Rolf Nussbaumer Photography/Alamy; 14–15, © xu wu/Getty Images; 16–17, © SOPA Images Limited/Alamy; 17, © RoschetzkyIstockPhoto/iStock; 18–19, © Satheesh Rajh Rajagopalan/Alamy; 20–21, © Marianne A. Campolongo/Alamy; 21, © wrangel/iStock; 22–23, © McGraw/Shutterstock; 24–25, © I. Noyan Yilmaz/Shutterstock; 26–27, © David Parker/Alamy; 28, © Sundry Photography/Shutterstock; 29 step 1, © Imagesines/iStock; 29 step 2, © terra24/iStock; 29 step 3, © FatCamera/iStock; 29 step 4, © AscentXmedia/iStock; and 29 step 5, © Kameleon007/iStock.

Bearport Publishing Company Product Development Team
President: Jen Jenson; Director of Product Development: Spencer Brinker; Senior Editor: Allison Juda; Editor: Charly Haley; Associate Editor: Naomi Reich; Senior Designer: Colin O'Dea; Associate Designer: Elena Klinkner; Associate Designer: Kayla Eggert; Product Development Assistant: Anita Stasson

Library of Congress Cataloging-in-Publication Data is available at www.loc.gov or upon request from the publisher.

ISBN: 979-8-88509-413-9 (hardcover)
ISBN: 979-8-88509-535-8 (paperback)
ISBN: 979-8-88509-650-8 (ebook)

For more information, write to Bearport Publishing, 5357 Penn Avenue South, Minneapolis, MN 55419.

Contents

A Connected World

At the edge of a freshwater pond, tall grasses wave in the breeze. A raccoon walks by, looking for bird eggs to eat, while a goose nibbles on a cattail and a frog munches on a dragonfly snack. Below the surface, fish dart through a forest of underwater plants. Buzzing, splashing, and swimming life is all around.

But some ponds are coated with a sticky green scum. Others have dried up completely, leaving dead plants and animals behind. What is happening to life on Earth?

Wetlands cover only 6 percent of Earth's surface, but 40 percent of the planet's plant and animal **species** live or make their babies within them.

A Planet Full of Life

Earth is made up of **biomes**—areas of land and sea where the **climate** and natural features allow certain kinds of plants and animals to live together. Oceans, forests, grasslands, deserts, tundras, and wetlands are all biomes.

Every biome is home to a connected community of plant and animal life. This wide variety of life is called **biodiversity**. A wetland biome can include everything from tiny **bacteria** and frogs to beavers and alligators. Each living thing plays a role in the survival of life within the biome.

One of the world's largest wetlands is in Bolivia—and it is the size of North Dakota! It is home to hundreds of species of mammals, birds, reptiles, amphibians, fish, and plants.

Beavers are wetland community builders! Their dams create new wetlands, ponds, and lakes.

It All Fits Together

The plants and animals within biomes form communities necessary for survival. They depend upon one another for the food, water, and shelter they need.

Leaves and stems from dead wetland plants are broken down by bacteria, creating **nutrients** that feed small water dwellers. Then, larger animals feed on the smaller ones. All of these creatures lay their eggs, raise their young, and live among the wetland plants that help keep the water clean by filtering out harmful pollution. It's a big, wet web of life!

Nutrients and plant material flushed from wetlands during storms provide food for other plants, fish, and wildlife living far downstream.

Water World

A wetland is a biome where the soil is usually covered in shallow water. Storm water from nearby lakes, rivers, and oceans flows into a wetland. The biome's plants draw the water in and then slowly release it.

Healthy wetlands are never totally dry. The plants that live in these biomes, such as ferns, rushes, and cattails, all thrive in water. Some plants live underwater, while the leaves and stems of others grow out above the waterline. Duckweed and other unrooted plants grow on the water's surface.

There are many kinds of wetlands, including freshwater swamps, bogs, marshes, and ponds. Saltwater wetlands can be found along the coastline.

A saltwater coastal wetland

Vanishing Wetlands

Wetlands are so packed with a wide variety of life that they have been called the ultimate biodiversity hotspot. Yet these biomes are in serious trouble. Over the last 300 years, almost 90 percent of the world's wetlands have disappeared. More than a third of the wetlands in the United States alone have vanished in the last 50 years, and globally more than a quarter of wetland plant and animal species are at risk of extinction. What is causing this loss?

About one-third of all threatened or **endangered** plant and animal species in the U.S. depend on wetlands for their survival.

Down the Drain

One leading cause of wetland destruction is **development**. Wetlands are often drained to make way for houses, businesses, and farms. People dig ditches that carry water away, drying the land to make it easier for this construction.

When a wetland is drained, beavers, deer, ducks, and other land-dwelling animals often leave to seek food and shelter elsewhere. But other animals, such as clams, snails, worms, and tortoises, can't relocate. They die off when the water disappears. Likewise, wetland **vegetation** is soon destroyed. That means the birds that rely on these plants no longer have shelter or nesting land.

The lower 48 American states lose 125 square miles (320 sq km) of wetlands every year. That's about about the size of seven football fields every hour!

No Flow

Other wetlands are destroyed by another kind of human construction—dams. These human-made structures are built to control the flow of rivers and to store water. Wetlands connected to rivers dry up when dams block the water and the flow is cut off. Without water, plants wither and fish lose both their homes and source of food. Then, birds no longer visit, and the animals that eat them must leave to avoid dying of hunger.

Once wetlands disappear, any water that used to be captured by wetland plants is left uncontrolled. Overflowing streams and ocean storm tides flood areas that used to remain dry thanks to wetlands.

Bad Blooms

We depend on farming for the food we eat, but sometimes this harms wetlands. Most farmers use chemical **fertilizers** to help crops grow. When it rains, these chemicals are washed into nearby wetlands, causing **algae** blooms. A burst of growth may seem like a good thing. But algae makes a thick scum on the water's surface, blocking the sunlight that wetland plants need. When these plants die, fish, birds, and other animals go hungry.

Some lake communities are planting wetland vegetation on floating platforms made of soil, foam, and recycled plastic. The plants' long roots soak up the chemicals that cause lake algae to bloom.

The huge amount of algae also uses up the oxygen in the water, **suffocating** the hungry fish. It can even release poisons that make other wetland animals sick.

A lake covered in red algae

Do You Belong Here?

Allowing fertilizer into a wetland causes lots of problems. But what harm could there be in introducing new plants? In the 1800s, a reed called a phragmite was brought to North America from Europe. This plant releases thousands of seeds each year, and its roots spread far and deep. It quickly took over many wetlands. Today, these **invasive** reeds overshadow, crowd out, and kill **native** wetland plants that provide critical food and shelter. When those plants disappear, so do many animals.

After Asian carp were introduced to North American wetlands, the invasive fish quickly began gobbling up all the food that many native species rely on for survival.

Too Salty!

Sometimes, things humans do result in harm to wetlands in unexpected ways. When people burn fuel, **carbon dioxide** is released. Once in the air, this gas traps heat around Earth, causing temperatures around the world to rise.

When water gets warmer, it takes up more space. This means that the same sea water reaches farther onto land. Some freshwater coastal wetlands are being flooded with ocean water. The salty water harms the roots of freshwater plants. They often die as a result.

Like some plants, many fish, frogs, and insects die when saltwater invades a wetland. The birds that snack on them go hungry and must leave to find food elsewhere.

People and Wetlands

If wetlands become unhealthy, so will we. Wetlands filter out pollutants, helping to keep rivers, bays, and oceans cleaner. Sometimes, we even use wetlands for drinking water.

For thousands of years, wetland plants have been used to make medicines. Even today, some people use them to treat everything from coughs, fevers, and rashes to headaches, diarrhea, and burns.

They are also important sources of the food we eat. Fish, berries, and rice all grow in these biomes. Wetland plants are a tasty—and healthy—treat for grazing farm animals, too. In turn, these cows, sheep, and goats feed people, providing us with meat and milk.

Wetland Life Returns

All around the world, people are realizing how important wetlands are to Earth. Healthy wetlands are being protected from development, and damaged ones are being replanted and restored. Farmers are switching to natural fertilizers and building new wetlands on their farms to trap pollution. Invasive plants are being removed, and rivers are being reconnected to wetlands to restore the safe flow of clean water. As wetlands come back, our planet becomes healthier for a wide variety of plants and animals.

The Everglades are a huge wetland in Florida. Unfortunately, the Everglades have been greatly damaged. A 35-year project is underway to restore this important wetland.

Wildlife scientists are working to clear toxic algae from some wetlands.

Save the Wetlands

Saving wetlands and the life they contain seems like a huge job. But there are small steps we can take to protect them and reduce the amount of heat-trapping carbon dioxide we put into the air.

Try to keep your yard healthy without chemical fertilizer or other chemicals that could run off into wetlands.

Keep sidewalks, lawns, and driveways clear of pet waste, trash, and motor oil. These things can wash into storm drains and end up in wetlands.

If you live in an area that is trying to restore a local wetland, join in to help clean up and add new plants.

Avoid using gas whenever you can. If possible and safe, walk, ride a bike, or take public transportation to get where you're going.

Electricity is often made by burning fuel. Save electricity by turning off lights when you're not using them. Also, unplug all devices and chargers when not in use.

Glossary

algae tiny plantlike living things that grow in water

bacteria tiny living things that live in water, soil, plants, and animals, and may cause illness

biodiversity the presence of many different kinds of plants and animals within an area

biomes regions with a particular climate and environment where certain kinds of plants and animals live

carbon dioxide a gas given off when fossil fuels are burned

climate the typical weather in a place

development the use of land for human activity, commonly including building new construction

endangered close to being killed or dying off completely

fertilizers substances added to soil to make plants grow better

invasive spreading in a place where something doesn't belong

native originally belonging to a certain place

nutrients vitamins, minerals, and other substances needed by living things for health and growth

species groups that animals and plants are divided into according to similar characteristics

suffocating experiencing a lack of oxygen

vegetation plant life

Read More

Bergin, Raymond. *Rising Seas (What on Earth? Climate Change Explained).* Minneapolis: Bearport Publishing Company, 2022.

Neuenfeldt, Elizabeth. *Wetlands Animals (What Animal Am I?).* Minneapolis: Bellwether Media, 2023.

Willis, John. *Wetlands (Aquatic Ecosystems).* New York: AV2, 2021.

Learn More Online

1. Go to **www.factsurfer.com** or scan the QR code below.

2. Enter "**Wetland Connections**" into the search box.

3. Click on the cover of this book to see a list of websites.

Index

About the Author

Raymond Bergin lives in New Jersey. One of his earliest memories is exploring a wetland near his house. Sadly, the wetland has since been drained to make way for a housing development.